Happy Alphabet Book

T0352861

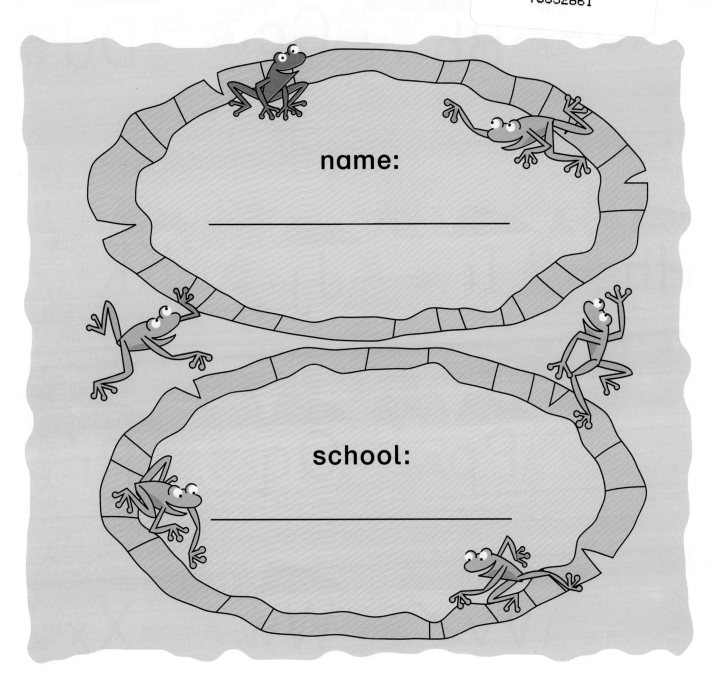

name:

_____

school:

_____

OXFORD
UNIVERSITY PRESS

● **Look at the alphabet**

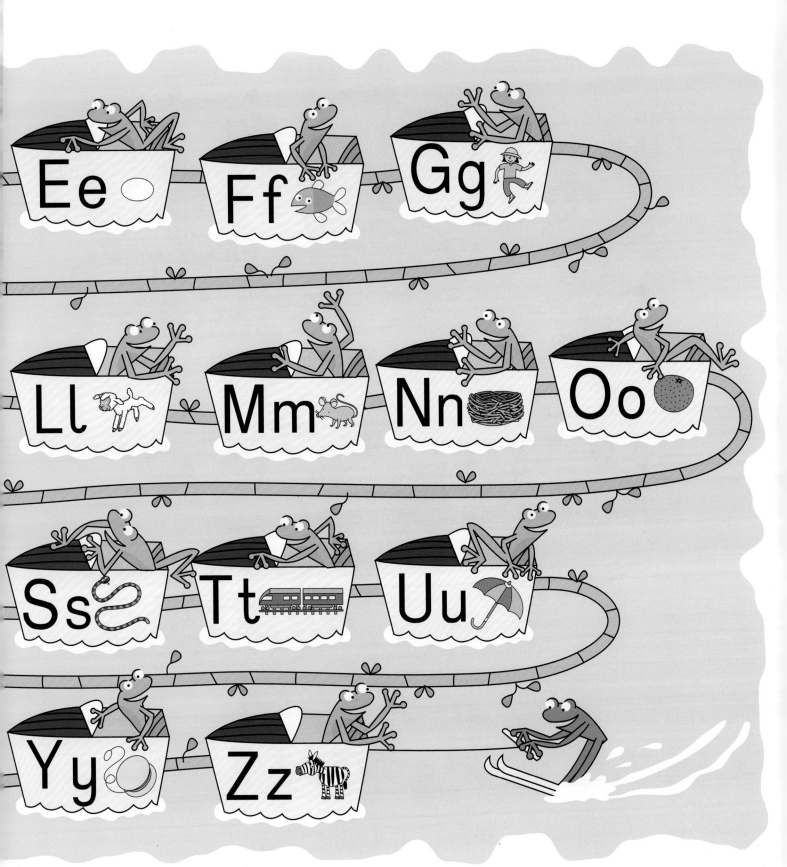

Look at the numbers

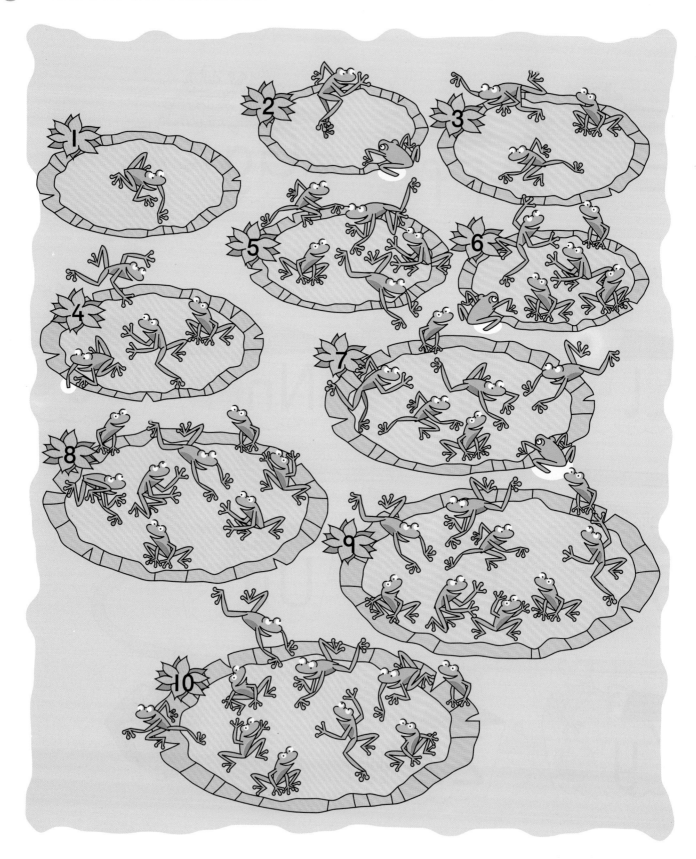

Draw Fred

Write

apple

Trace

a a a a

Copy

boy

Trace

b b b b

Copy

Write

cat

Trace

C   C   C   C

Copy

dog

Trace

d   d   d   d

Copy

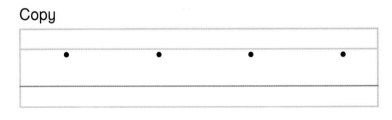

Write

egg

fish

Trace

Copy

Trace

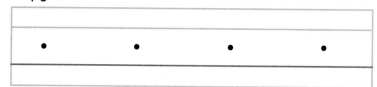

Copy

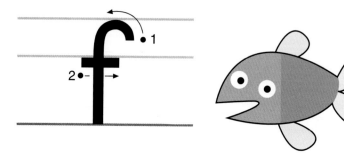

Write

girl

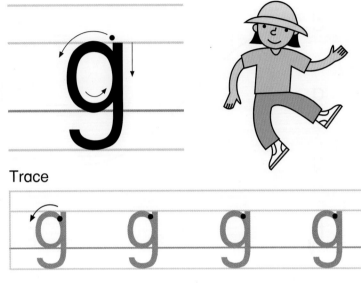

g

Trace

g   g   g   g

Copy

hat

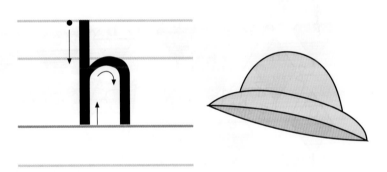

h

Trace

h   h   h   h

Copy

9

Match and write

d

g

a

f

_ i r l

_ i s h

<u>d</u> o g

_ p p l e

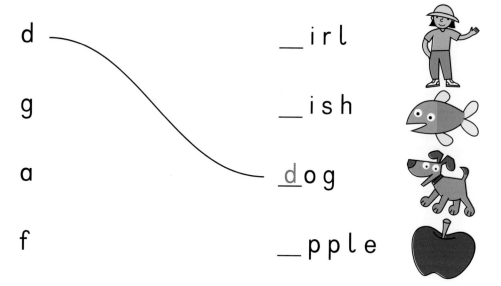

Find and count

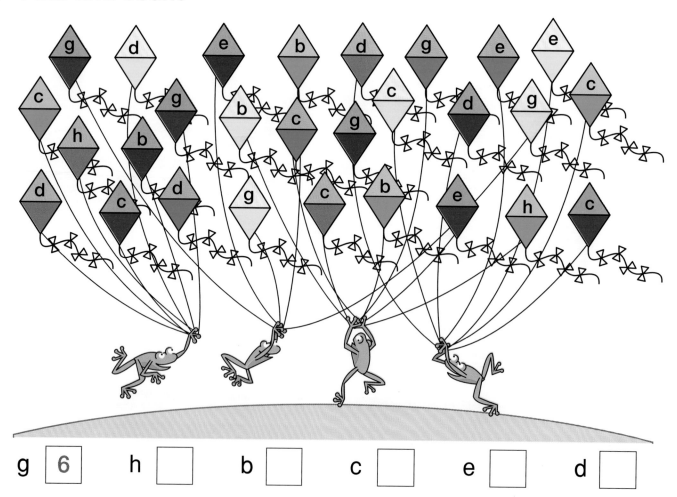

| g | 6 | h | | b | | c | | e | | d | |

Match and colour

fish

egg

hat

boy

Choose and tick ✓

egg ☐	apple ✓
boy ☐	girl ☐
cat ☐	dog ☐
fish ☐	hat ☐

Write

ice cream

i

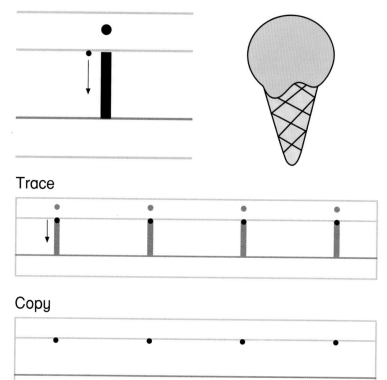

Trace

Copy

jeans

j

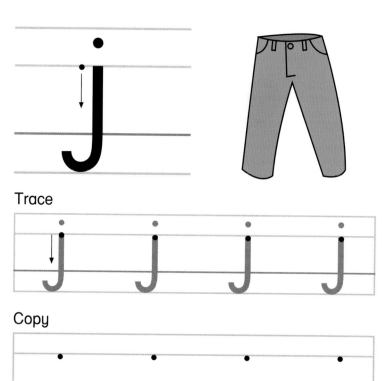

Trace

Copy

Write

kite

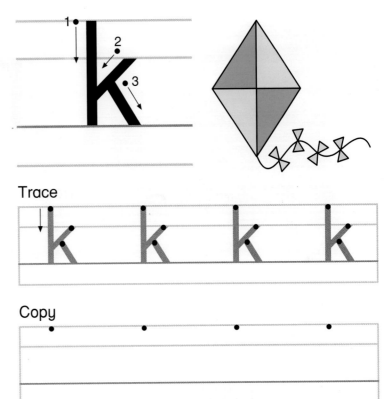

Trace

k k k k

Copy

lamb

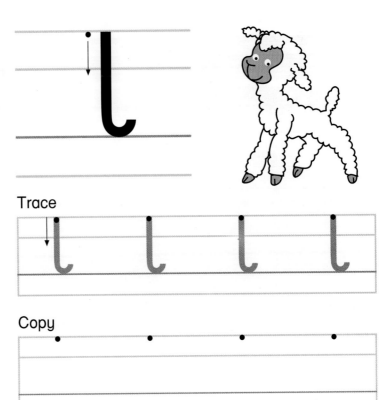

Trace

Copy

13

Write

mouse

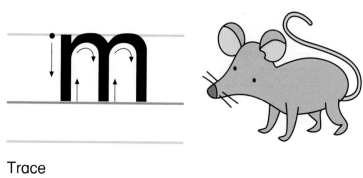

Trace

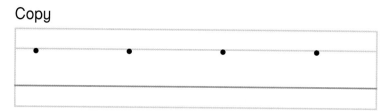

Copy

nest

Trace

Copy

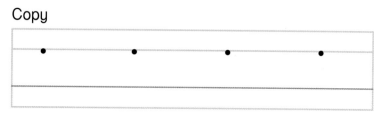

Write

orange

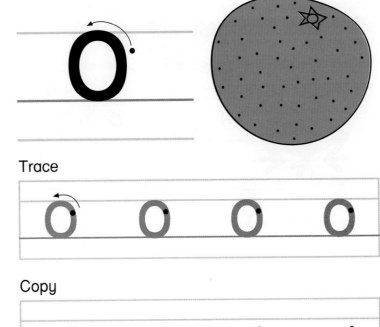

o

Trace

o o o o

Copy

• • • •

plane

p

Trace

p p p p

Copy

• • • •

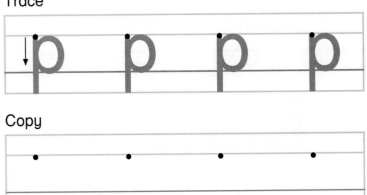

15

Write

n p a l e

p l

p l a n e

g o d

a e l p p

g e g

m l b a

Find and count

b [2]　p [　]　o [　]　c [　]　h [　]　g [　]

Circle

d	j	c	f	i	s	h	e
o	e	r	n	a	s	t	g
l	a	a	p	p	y	e	g
a	n	b	a	p	p	l	e
m	s	b	o	n	h	u	t
b	n	o	s	k	i	t	e
x	a	y	k	i	t	t	w
n	e	s	t	w	u	l	f

Write

queen

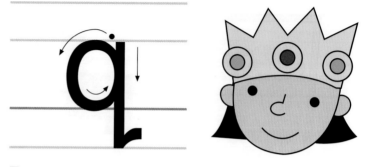

Trace

Copy

rabbit

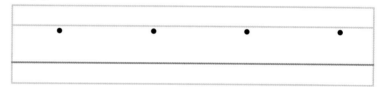

Trace

Copy

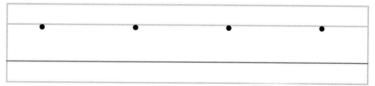

Write

snake

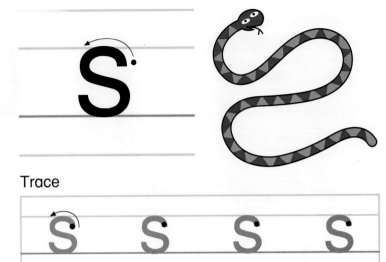

S

Trace

S S S S

Copy

• • • •

train

t

1
2

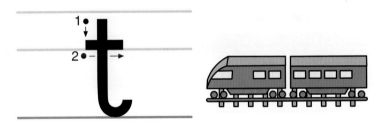

Trace

t t t t

Copy

• • • •

umbrella

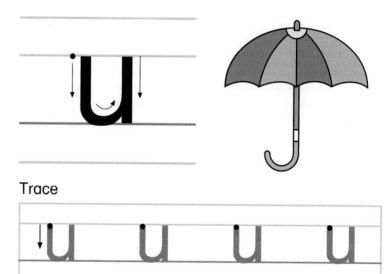

Trace

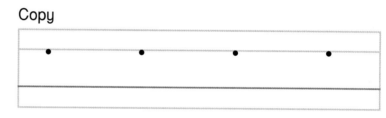

Copy

violin

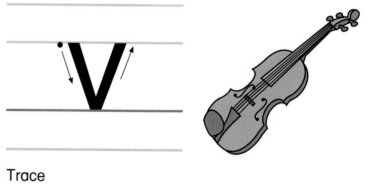

Trace

Copy

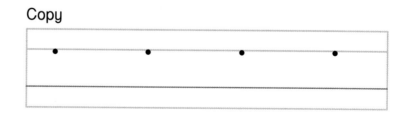

● Write

wolf

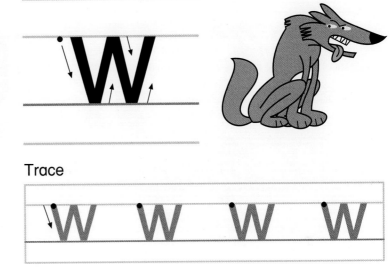

Trace

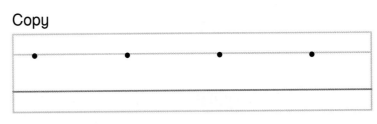

Copy

fox

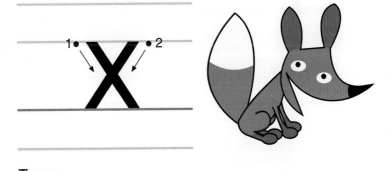

Trace

Copy

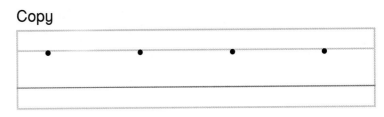

Write

yoyo

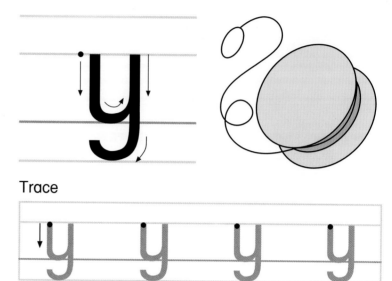

Trace

Copy

zebra

Trace

Copy

Write

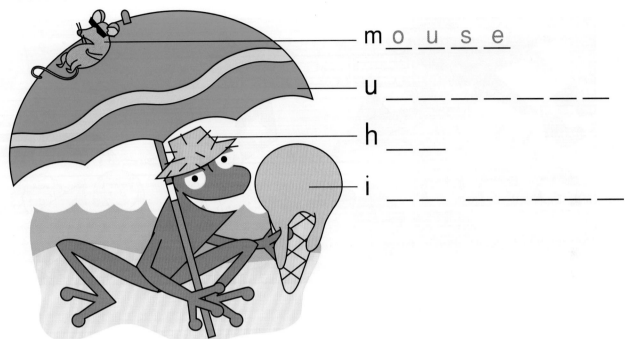

m <u>o</u> <u>u</u> <u>s</u> <u>e</u>

u _ _ _ _ _ _ _ _

h _ _

i _ _ _ _ _ _

Write

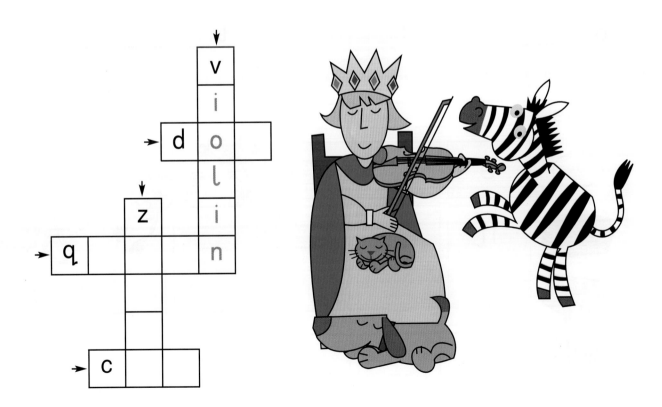

● Find, write, and count

g <u>i</u> <u>r</u> <u>l</u> | 4 |

b _ _ | |

k _ _ _ | |

y _ _ _ | |

p _ _ _ _ | |

t _ _ _ _ | |

● Write

● Find, write, and count the animals

c a t _____ | 7 |

f _____ | |

d _____ | |

l _____ | |

s _____ | |

r _____ | |

m _____ | |

w _____ | |

Write

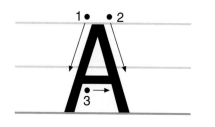

a

Trace, then copy

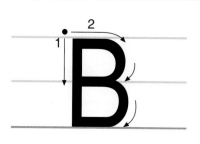

b

Trace, then copy

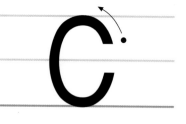

c

Trace, then copy

Write

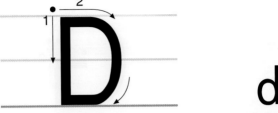

d

Trace, then copy

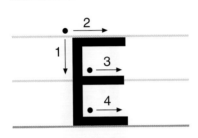

e

Trace, then copy

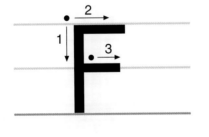

f

Trace, then copy

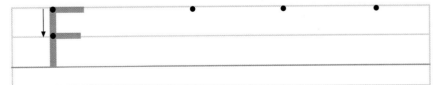

Write

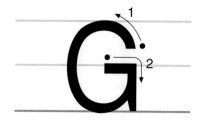

g

Trace, then copy

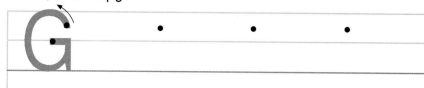

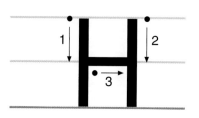

h

Trace, then copy

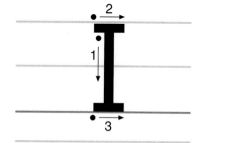

i

Trace, then copy

Write

j

Trace, then copy

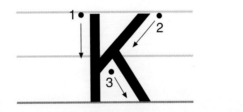

k

Trace, then copy

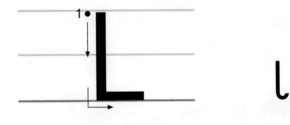

l

Trace, then copy

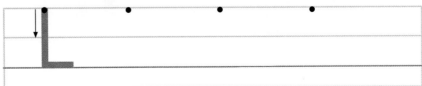

Match and write

Match and colour

Colour and count the eggs

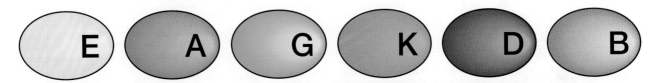

A | I | G | | E | | K | | B | | D | |

Match and colour

Write

m

Trace, then copy

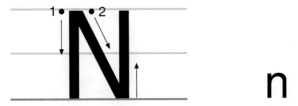

n

Trace, then copy

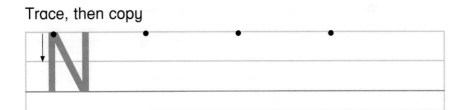

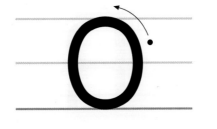

o

Trace, then copy

Write

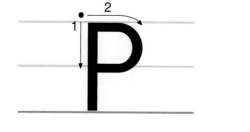

p

Trace, then copy

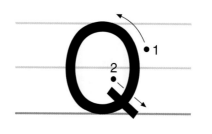

q

Trace, then copy

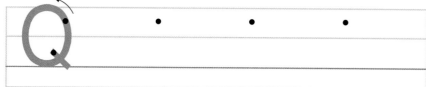

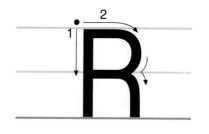

r

Trace, then copy

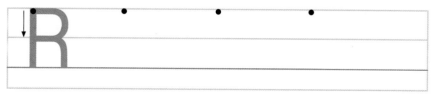

Write

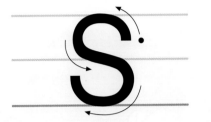

s

Trace, then copy

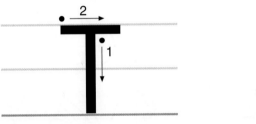

t

Trace, then copy

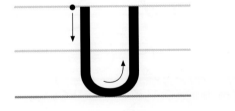

u

Trace, then copy

Match and colour

Match and colour

● Write

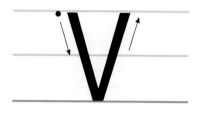

V

Trace, then copy

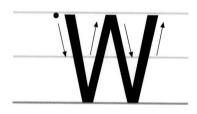

W

Trace, then copy

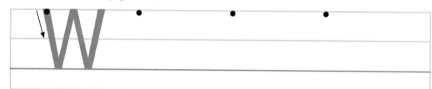

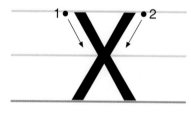

X

Trace, then copy

Write

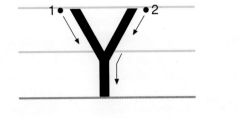

Trace, then copy

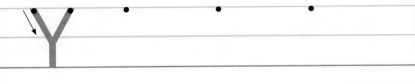

y

z

Trace, then copy

● **Match and colour**

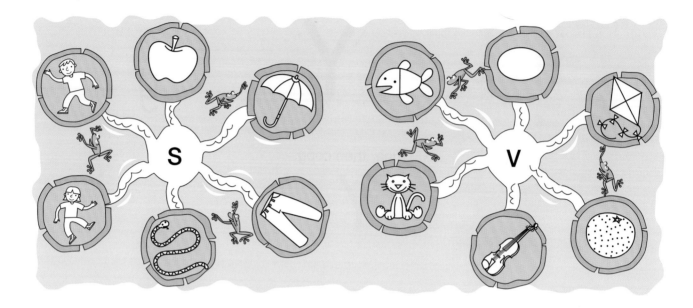

● **Count**

O	10	W		S		V	
U		Y		X		Z	

Colour the alphabet path and find the rabbit

Write the alphabet

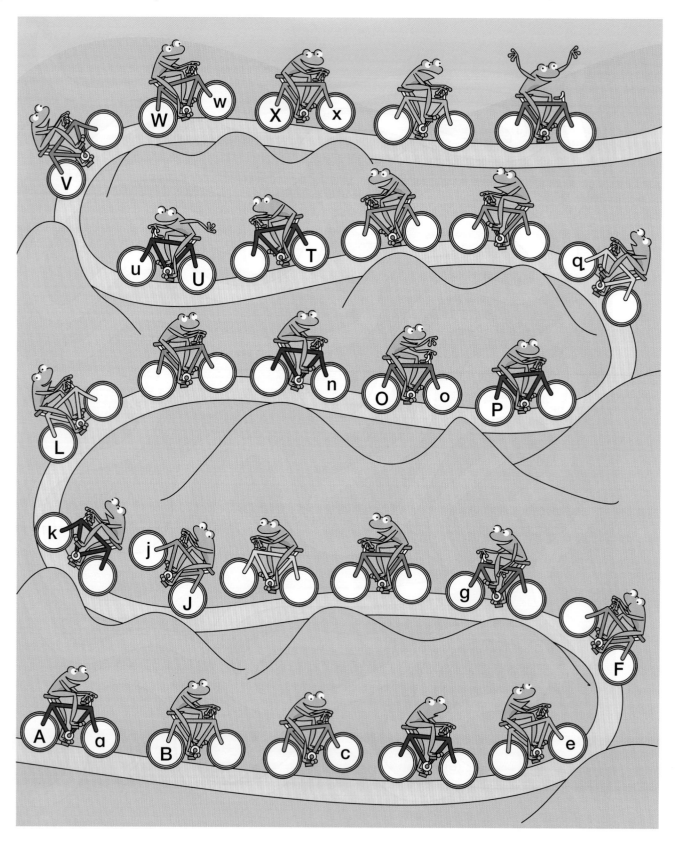

Write the words in order

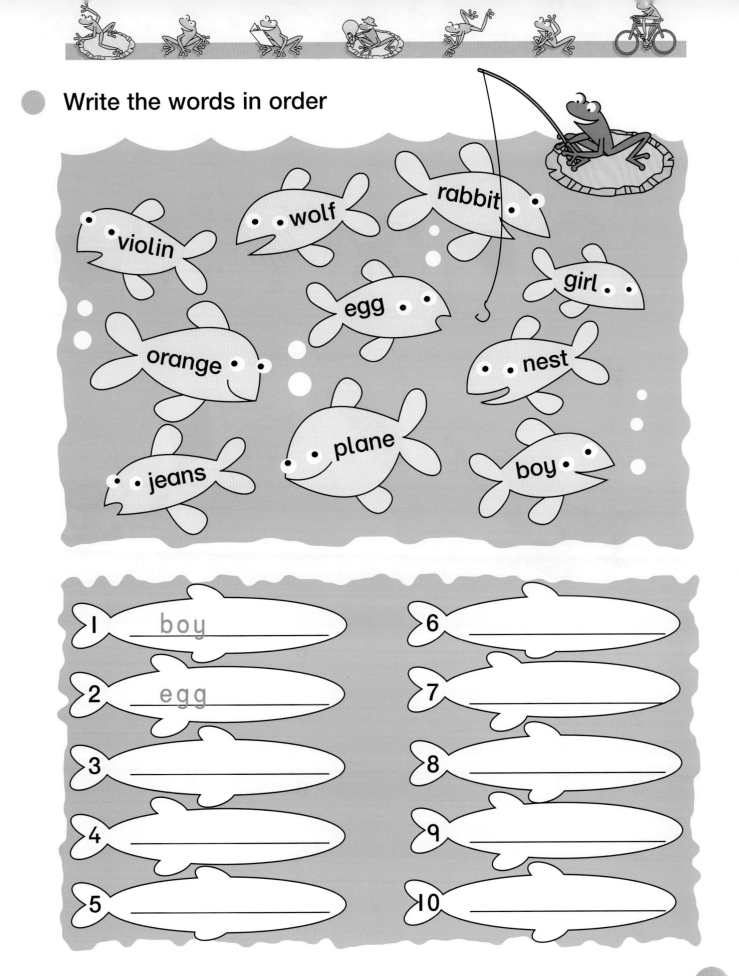

violin • wolf • rabbit • girl • egg • orange • nest • jeans • plane • boy

1 boy

2 egg

3 _____

4 _____

5 _____

6 _____

7 _____

8 _____

9 _____

10 _____

Write the words in order

1 apple	6
2 cat	7
3	8
4	9
5	10

Write my name

F _ _ _ _   _ _ _ g

Find Fred

TEACHER'S NOTES

The aim of *Happy Alphabet Book* is to help children to recognize and write the letters of the roman alphabet, using the correct hand movement. The children start by tracing and copying the lower-case letters. Each letter is linked to a picture to help them to practise the sound. These letters and words are then practised in exercises. The children then trace and copy the upper-case letters. (The corresponding lower-case letters are also given so that the children can recognize and link the lower and upper case.) The children practise the upper-case letters in exercises. Then the whole alphabet is practised in a variety of exercises.

Before the children trace a letter, make sure they understand the word. Then demonstrate the letter on the board, explaining in the mother tongue what you are doing. The children start each tracing or copying movement on the dot provided.

Title page The children write their name and school in English.

Pages 2–3 Look at the alphabet Read through the alphabet with the children. Draw attention to the objects on the side of the boats but do not spend time teaching them.

Page 4 Look at the numbers The children count the frogs on each lily pad. Point to the number in the waterlily and say the word. The children repeat.

Page 5 Draw Fred The children join two sets of dots in numerical order to complete the picture. The red dots form one back leg and the blue dots form the other.

Pages 6–9 Write The children trace and copy the lower-case letters *a–h*.

Page 10 Match and write The children write the missing first letter to complete each illustrated word. (Answers: dog, girl, apple, fish) **Find and count** The children count the numbers of the lower-case letters in the kites. (Answers: g–6, h–2, b–4, c–7, e–4, d–5)

Page 11 Match and colour The children follow and colour the path from the objects on the left to the words on the right. **Choose and tick √** The children identify each picture and tick the box next to the correct word. (Answers: apple, boy, cat, hat)

Pages 12–15 Write The children trace and copy the lower-case letters *i–p*.

Page 16 Write The children identify the object in each of Fred's thought bubbles and write the letters in the correct order. (Answers: plane, dog, apple, egg, lamb)

Page 17 Find and count The children count the objects beginning with the letters given and write the number in the box. (Answers: b(oy)–2, p(lane)–5, o(range)–10, c(at)–7, h(at)–4, g(irl)–3) **Circle** The children circle the words (horizontal and vertical) that correspond with the pictures. (Answers: horizontal fish, apple, kite, nest; vertical lamb, jeans, boy, egg)

Pages 18–22 Write The children trace and copy the lower-case letters *q–z*.

Page 23 Write The children complete the words for each of the objects. (Answers: mouse, umbrella, hat, ice cream) **Write** The children look at the picture and complete the crossword. (Answers: vertical violin, zebra; horizontal dog, queen, cat)

Page 24 Find, write, and count The children count each kind of toy and person in the picture. They complete the word and write the number in the box. (Answers: girl–4, kite–6, plane–5, boy–3, yoyo–7, train–2) **Write** The children complete the wall with words that correspond to the pictures. (Answers: egg, nest, jeans, orange)

Page 25 Find, write, and count the animals The children count each kind of animal in the picture. They complete the word and write the number in the box. (Answers: cat–7, dog–4, snake–3, mouse–5, fish–10, lamb–8, rabbit–9, wolf–1)

Pages 26–29 Write The children trace and copy the upper-case letters *A–L*.

Page 30 Match and write The children match the large and small frogs by the colour of their hats. They write the corresponding upper-case letters at the top of the large frogs' hats.

Page 31 Match and colour The children decide which object is represented by the letter and colour the object. (Answers: pictures of dog and hat) **Colour and count the eggs** The children colour the small eggs in the picture in the same colours as the large eggs above. Then they count the small eggs. (Answers: A–1, G–7, E–4, K–2, B–5, D–3)

Page 32 Match and colour The children find each pair of large and small frogs with matching upper- and lower-case letters. They colour the T-shirts of each pair in the same colour.

Pages 33–35 Write The children trace and copy the upper-case letters *M–U*.

Page 36 Match and colour The children find each pair of large and small frogs with matching upper- and lower-case letters. They colour the caps of each pair in the same colour.

Page 37 Match and colour The children find each pair of large and small frogs with matching upper- and lower-case letters. They colour the scarves of each pair in the same colour.

Pages 38–39   **Write**   The children trace and copy the upper-case letters *V–Z*.

Page 40   **Match and colour**   The children decide which object is represented by the letter and colour the object. (Answers: pictures of snake and violin)   **Count**   The children count the numbers of upper-case letters in the picture. Note that the three balloons count as Os. (Answers: O–10, W–5, S–10, V–9, U–3, Y–2, X–8, Z–6)

Page 41   **Colour the alphabet path and find the rabbit**   The children colour in the path of the alphabet, choosing the correct letter at each junction.

Page 42   **Write the alphabet**   The children write the missing upper- and lower-case letters in the bicycle wheels. Tell them that the lower-case letter is always in the front wheel and the upper-case letter in the back wheel.

Page 43   **Write the words in order**   The children write the words in alphabetical order. (Answers: boy, egg, girl, jeans, nest, orange, plane, rabbit, violin, wolf)

Page 44   **Write the words in order**   The children identify the objects in the picture and write the words in alphabetical order. (Answers: apple, cat, dog, hat, kite, lamb, mouse, train, yoyo, zebra)

Page 45   **Write my name**   The children complete the name (Answer: Fred Frog)   **Find Fred**   The children look for Fred in the picture. Then they find all the lower-case letters, in alphabetical order.

OXFORD

UNIVERSITY PRESS

Great Clarendon Street, Oxford OX2 6DP

Oxford University Press is a department of the University of Oxford.
It furthers the University's objective of excellence in research, scholarship,
and education by publishing worldwide in

Oxford New York

Auckland Cape Town Dar es Salaam Hong Kong Karachi
Kuala Lumpur Madrid Melbourne Mexico City Nairobi
New Delhi Shanghai Taipei Toronto

With offices in

Argentina Austria Brazil Chile Czech Republic France Greece
Guatemala Hungary Italy Japan Poland Portugal Singapore
South Korea Switzerland Thailand Turkey Ukraine Vietnam

OXFORD and OXFORD ENGLISH are registered trade marks of
Oxford University Press in the UK and in certain other countries

ISBN : 978 0 19 433305 4

Designed and typeset by Oxford Designers & Illustrators

Printed in China

ACKNOWLEDGEMENT

Illustrations by John Haslam